70p

# *Sunlit Summits*
## PATIENCE STRONG

Frederick Muller Ltd
London

## Sunlit Summits

Things look difficult and dire – if no dream
spurs, and no desire – prods you on to scale
the crags – when faith grows faint and
will-power flags.

What do you wish for all the time? Press
on, work hard, prepare to climb – the
stairway of the rocky slopes – that wind
round the mountain of your hopes . . . The
summits that frown where the cloud veils
drop – smile on the man who can reach the
top.

# Rose-tinted Glasses

Put on your rose-tinted glasses. A soft rosy
glow you will see – around the dark cloud
as it passes. A different world it could be –
if everyone looked at their troubles
through lenses that brighten the day – The
troubles would soon turn to bubbles – that
quickly go floating away.

It may be a visual deception – but try it. It
works; this I know . . . Life takes on
another complexion – when seen through
a roseate glow.

# *Hallelujah Chorus*

Every upward-thrusting bud that bursts
out into bloom – is a living symbol of the
rising from the tomb – bringing life and
light and love to all with eyes to see – the
meaning and the glory of the Cross of
Calvary . . . And every bird that sings its
Easter anthem to the spring – swells the
Hallelujah chorus sung to Christ the King.

# *You Said . . .*

You said one should never look backward
– but there I sat day after day – dredging
the pools of remembrance – for something
to carry away – Something of joy for my
comfort – but no comfort there did I find –
only the ache of old sorrows – and
shadows that darkened the mind.

And so I looked forward, believing in a
future not wholly bereft – of hope in a new
kind of living – redeeming the years that
were left . . . Now thankful am I that I took
that new track. You were right when you
said you should never look back.

## *Burdens and Blessings*

You will never lack a burden. When you think at last you're free – you will find new burdens waiting – That's the way it has to be. If you see the needs of others as you travel life's rough road – you will never lack a burden – there'll be someone else's load – to ease, to carry or to share. The burden-bearing never ends – but you will gain what you have given when you come to count your friends.

## Live Out Your Dreams

Happy you looked on that wonderful day
– when you walked down the aisle with
your bridal bouquet – But did you, by any
chance, hear someone say – it would be
roses and cream all the way? . . . Of course
not; you ought to have known then and
there – that marriage means learning to
build and to share – working at making
your home a success – giving and taking;
that's life . . . more or less.

And here you are wishing you two hadn't
met. What did you think you were going
to get – Heaven on earth without passing
the test? Run home, and weigh up the
worst with the best. Bury the grievance –
your promise renew. Live out your dream
and your dream will come true.

# *Passing Over*

The storm did not break as you dreaded –
The black-hooded clouds moved away . . .
They were only passing over – and it
turned out a beautiful day . . . The things
that you fear seldom happen – though
mountains obscure the far light – they fade
away as you approach them – Beyond all is
well, all is bright. So cling to your faith for
the future, Hold fast to the hopes that
destroy – the shadows that darken your
threshold – the phantoms that threaten
your joy.

## *From Now On*

From now on I resolve to climb – just one
mountain at a time – to solve the problems
as they come – reducing the minimum –
the strain of trying in advance – to foresee
every circumstance.

From now on go on quietly – leaving to the
powers that be – the outcome of the day's
events. It is only common sense . . . Why
rush to meet what's out of sight?
Tomorrow all things may come right.
Today's race is the race to run. Fight your
battles one by one.

# *Both Ways*

You can't have it both ways and that is
because – it's not in accordance with life's
basic laws. You can't eat your cake and
enjoy the same slice – at teatime
tomorrow; you can't eat it twice.

You'll never be trusted when once it is
found – you run with the hare and you
hunt with the hound. You must not
complain over bills on the mat – if money
you've squandered on this and on that . . .
You can't walk due east with your eyes on
the west. You have to decide what is right,
what is best.

## Lost in Thought

Sometimes when you're lost in thought
you find a new way through – all the
worries and the problems that are
troubling you . . . Cease to work the tiller,
drifting blind, and suddenly – you are at
the longed-for haven where your heart
would be. You have to lose yourself to find
the treasure you have lost. You have to
trust the water whether calm or
tempest-tossed – to take you to the truth
that you with toil and tears have sought.
Great discoveries are made when you are
lost in thought.

# Up There

If you want the rain, you have to put up
with the cloud – for clouds bring
benefaction to the earth . . . Do not
grumble when they come the blue sky to
enshroud – for they put an end to drought
and dearth.

Clouds pour out their blessings on the
country and the town – sustaining life
upon the living lands – Man conserves –
but cannot make the water flowing down –
from Heaven. It's a gift from unseen
hands.

So we have to look up there for our most
vital need. Perhaps we're not so clever after
all! . . . It is rain that fills the wells and
swells the growing seed – So receive it
gladly. Let it fall.

## Between the Sunshine and the Showers

You'll never see a rainbow in a clear
unbroken sky. They come in storm, but
never stay. The clouds in passing by – drop
the rain that makes the glory where the sun
rays glow – over-arching earth and heaven
with a seven-hued bow.

The smiles that are the loveliest are those
upon a face – on which the tears have fallen
when a joy comes to replace – the sorrow
in a heart grown sad with hard uphappy
hours. Smiles are rainbows coming out
between the sun and showers.

# *To All Men Everywhere*

You'll never see a rainbow if your eyes are
blurred with tears. You'll never climb a
mountain if your heart is faint with fears.
You'll never reach the top rung on the
ladder to the stars – You'll never have the
strength to break through barriers and bars
– unless you have inside you the capacity to
see – yourself as God's own child within
the human family.

You are the appointed one, the beneficiary.
Christ redeemed and bought you on the
hill of Calvary – offspring of the seed of
faith, the royal and rightful heir – which
makes you brother through His love to all
men everywhere.

## Remember the Best

There are days when the world is against
you. There are moments when nothing
goes right – when a heavy cloud seems to
surround you and you cannot get through
to the light. When you feel that your
courage is sagging it's not easy to work up
a smile – There are rough bits of road on all
journeys – for it couldn't be smooth all the
while. But when thinking of all your
misfortunes – think too of how much
you've been blessed . . . Don't brood on the
worst that has happened and fail to
remember the best.